Chasing Shadows:

A Guide to the April 8 Total Solar Eclipse

NOAH J. A.

Table of Contents

INTRODUCTION

Overview of the April 8 Total Solar Eclipse:

The April 8 total solar eclipse is set to be one of the most anticipated astronomical events of the year. On this day, the moon will align perfectly between the Earth and the sun, casting its shadow across a significant swath of North America. The path of totality, where the sun will be completely obscured by the moon, will stretch from the Pacific Northwest through the central United States and into the

Southeast, providing a rare celestial spectacle for millions of observers.

The total solar eclipse will begin its journey across the Earth's surface in the early morning hours, starting in the Pacific Ocean before making landfall along the coast of Oregon. From there, it will traverse eastward, passing over states such as Idaho, Montana, Wyoming, Nebraska, and Kansas, before exiting the continental United States over the Gulf Coast of Texas and Louisiana. Along the approximately 2700-mile path, lucky spectators within the path of totality will experience moments of complete darkness in the middle of the day as the moon completely blocks out the sun.

For those outside the path of totality, a partial solar eclipse will still be visible across a broader region, providing a unique opportunity to witness a celestial alignment, albeit with less dramatic effects than those within the path of totality. Regardless of location, the April 8 total solar eclipse promises to be a memorable event for skywatchers, scientists, and enthusiasts alike.

Significance of Solar Eclipses:

Solar eclipses have captivated human imagination for centuries, serving as awe-inspiring reminders of the dynamic interactions between the Earth, moon, and sun. Beyond their inherent beauty, solar eclipses hold significant scientific, cultural, and historical importance.

From a scientific standpoint, solar eclipses offer researchers valuable opportunities to study the sun's outer atmosphere, known as the corona, which is typically obscured by the sun's intense glare. During a total solar eclipse, when the moon fully blocks the sun's bright disk, the corona becomes visible as a glowing halo surrounding the darkened sun. This rare glimpse into the sun's outer layers provides scientists with crucial data to better understand solar phenomena and space weather dynamics.

Culturally and historically, solar eclipses have held profound significance for civilizations around the world. Ancient cultures often interpreted eclipses as omens or celestial messages, leading to various myths, rituals, and traditions associated with these celestial events. Today, solar eclipses continue to inspire wonder and fascination, drawing people together to witness the grandeur of nature's cosmic ballet.

Moreover, solar eclipses serve as opportunities for education and outreach, encouraging public engagement with science and astronomy. Through organized viewing events, educational programs, and citizen science initiatives, solar eclipses provide platforms for learning and discovery, inspiring future generations of scientists, astronomers, and sky enthusiasts.

In summary, the April 8 total solar eclipse represents not only a spectacular celestial event but also a reminder of humanity's enduring curiosity and connection to the cosmos. As millions of eyes turn skyward to witness this natural phenomenon, the significance of solar eclipses as windows into the wonders of the universe becomes ever more apparent.

UNDERSTANDING SOLAR ECLIPSES

What Causes a Solar Eclipse?

Solar eclipses occur when the moon, in its orbit around the Earth, passes between the Earth and the sun, resulting in the temporary blocking or obscuring of the sun's light. This alignment of the sun, moon, and Earth must be precise for a solar eclipse to occur. There are two primary types of solar eclipses: total and partial.

- **Total Solar Eclipse:** During a total solar eclipse, the moon completely covers the sun's disk, creating a brief period of darkness known as totality. This phenomenon occurs when the apparent size of the moon matches or exceeds that of the sun, allowing it to completely block the sun's light. Total solar eclipses are relatively rare events that occur only along narrow paths on the Earth's surface. Observers within the path of totality experience the full spectacle of the sun's corona, the sun's outer atmosphere, which is typically hidden from view by the sun's glare.

2. **Partial Solar Eclipse:** A partial solar eclipse occurs when only a portion of the sun's disk is obscured by the moon as viewed from Earth. In this scenario, the alignment of the sun, moon, and Earth is such that the moon only partially covers the sun, creating a crescent-shaped pattern in the sky. Partial solar eclipses are more common than total eclipses and can be observed from a broader geographic area. However, the level of obscuration varies depending on the observer's location relative to the path of the eclipse.

The occurrence of solar eclipses is governed by the orbital dynamics of the Earth and moon. Because the moon's orbit is inclined relative to the Earth's orbit around the sun, solar eclipses do not happen every month. Instead, they occur only during specific alignment periods known as eclipse seasons, which typically happen twice a year. Additionally, the apparent size of the moon can vary slightly due to its elliptical orbit around the Earth, affecting the likelihood of a total solar eclipse versus a partial eclipse.

Solar eclipses are remarkable celestial events that provide unique opportunities for scientific study, public engagement, and cultural significance. Understanding the mechanics behind solar eclipses enhances our appreciation for these awe-inspiring phenomena and deepens our understanding of the complex interactions between the Earth, moon, and sun.

Types of Solar Eclipses

Solar eclipses come in various types, depending on the alignment of the sun, moon, and Earth, as well as the observer's location. The primary types of solar eclipses include:

1. **Total Solar Eclipse:** As described earlier, a total solar eclipse occurs when the moon completely blocks the sun's disk, resulting in a brief period of darkness known as totality. Total solar eclipses are relatively rare events that captivate observers with their stunning visual effects, including the appearance of the sun's corona.

2. **Partial Solar Eclipse:** During a partial solar eclipse, only a portion of

the sun's disk is obscured by the moon as viewed from Earth. This occurs when the alignment of the sun, moon, and Earth is such that the moon partially covers the sun, creating a crescent-shaped pattern in the sky. Partial solar eclipses are more common than total eclipses and can be observed from a broader geographic area.

3. **Annular Solar Eclipse:** An annular solar eclipse occurs when the moon passes directly in front of the sun but does not completely cover it. Instead, a ring of sunlight, known as

the "ring of fire," surrounds the darkened silhouette of the moon. This phenomenon happens when the moon is near its apogee, the farthest point from Earth in its elliptical orbit, causing it to appear slightly smaller in diameter than the sun.

4. **Hybrid Solar Eclipse:** A hybrid solar eclipse, also known as an annular-total eclipse, is a rare type of eclipse that transitions between a total and annular eclipse along its path of totality. This occurs due to variations in the Earth's curvature, causing observers at different locations along

the eclipse path to experience different types of eclipses. Hybrid eclipses are relatively uncommon and offer a unique viewing experience for those fortunate enough to be within the path of totality.

Each type of solar eclipse provides observers with distinct visual phenomena and viewing experiences, ranging from the dramatic darkness of a total eclipse to the ethereal "ring of fire" of an annular eclipse. Regardless of the type, solar eclipses serve as reminders of the dynamic interactions between celestial bodies and offer opportunities for scientific study, cultural significance, and public engagement.

THE PATH OF TOTALITY

Route and Duration of the April 8 Eclipse:

The April 8 total solar eclipse will cast its shadow across a significant swath of North America, providing a thrilling celestial spectacle for observers along its path of totality. The eclipse will begin its journey in the early morning hours over the Pacific Ocean before making landfall along the coast of Oregon. From there, it will traverse eastward across the United States, passing over several states before exiting the mainland over the Gulf Coast of Texas and Louisiana.

The total solar eclipse will follow a path approximately 2700 miles long, with its duration varying depending on the observer's location within the path of totality. At its maximum duration, the eclipse will last for approximately 4 minutes and 28 seconds, making it one of the longest total solar eclipses in recent history. However, the duration of totality decreases gradually as one moves away from the central line of the eclipse path.

Observers situated within the central regions of the eclipse path will experience the longest duration of totality, while those located near the path's edges will witness shorter periods of darkness. Despite these variations, the April 8 total solar eclipse promises to deliver an unforgettable astronomical event for millions of spectators across North America.

Best Viewing Locations:

Several factors determine the best viewing locations for the April 8 total solar eclipse, including weather conditions, accessibility, and the duration of totality. While the eclipse will be visible from various regions along its path, some locations offer particularly advantageous viewing opportunities:

1. **Pacific Northwest:** Coastal areas of Oregon, including cities such as Newport, Lincoln City, and Depoe Bay, provide excellent vantage points for witnessing the eclipse as it makes landfall over the United States. These locations offer unobstructed views of the western horizon, allowing

observers to witness the eclipse's early stages as the moon's shadow approaches.

2. **Central United States:** States such as Idaho, Montana, Wyoming, and Nebraska lie directly in the path of totality, offering numerous viewing options for experiencing the eclipse. Cities like Boise (Idaho), Casper (Wyoming), and Lincoln (Nebraska) are popular destinations for eclipse enthusiasts seeking optimal viewing conditions and amenities.

3. **Southeast:** As the eclipse progresses eastward, cities in the Southeastern United States, including Nashville (Tennessee), Columbia (South Carolina), and Raleigh (North Carolina), will witness the phenomenon later in the morning. These locations provide opportunities for observers to experience totality and participate in organized viewing events and festivities.

4. **Gulf Coast:** Coastal areas of Texas and Louisiana mark the eclipse's final landfall before it moves out over the Gulf of Mexico. While totality

durations may be shorter in these regions, they offer unique viewing experiences for residents and visitors alike.

When selecting a viewing location, it is essential to consider factors such as accessibility, accommodations, and weather forecasts. Additionally, observers should take precautions to ensure their safety during the eclipse, including using certified solar viewing glasses and avoiding looking directly at the sun without proper eye protection.

Overall, the April 8 total solar eclipse presents a rare opportunity for skywatchers across North America to witness one of nature's most awe-inspiring phenomena. By choosing the best viewing locations and preparing accordingly, observers can maximize their chances of experiencing this celestial spectacle in all its glory.

SAFETY PRECAUTIONS

How to Safely Watch a Solar Eclipse:

Watching a solar eclipse can be an exhilarating experience, but it's crucial to prioritize safety to protect your eyes from potential harm. Directly viewing the sun, even during an eclipse, can cause permanent eye damage or blindness if proper precautions are not taken. Here are some essential safety tips for observing a solar eclipse:

1. **Use Certified Solar Viewing Glasses:** Invest in a pair of solar

viewing glasses that meet the ISO 12312-2 safety standard. These glasses are specifically designed to filter out harmful ultraviolet, visible, and infrared radiation from the sun, allowing you to safely view solar phenomena, including eclipses. Ensure that your glasses are in good condition, without any scratches, bends, or damage to the lenses.

2. **Never Look Directly at the Sun:** Never look directly at the sun with your naked eyes, binoculars, telescopes, or cameras without proper solar filters. Even during a partial

eclipse, the sun's intense rays can cause irreparable damage to your eyes within seconds. Always use certified solar viewing glasses or other approved viewing methods to observe the eclipse safely.

3. **Use Solar Filters for Optical Devices:** If you plan to use binoculars, telescopes, or cameras to observe the eclipse, ensure that they are equipped with solar filters specifically designed for solar viewing. These filters should be securely attached to the front of the optical device to block harmful radiation from

the sun. Do not use improvised filters or homemade solutions, as they may not provide adequate protection.

4. **Project the Image:** Another safe way to view a solar eclipse is by projecting the sun's image onto a surface using a pinhole projector or a telescope/binoculars. To create a pinhole projector, poke a small hole in a piece of cardboard and hold it up to the sun, allowing the sunlight to pass through the hole and project an image onto a surface below. Alternatively, use a telescope or binoculars to project

the sun's image onto a white screen or wall.

5. **Monitor Children and Pets:** Supervise children and pets during the eclipse to ensure that they do not accidentally look at the sun without proper eye protection. Educate them about the dangers of directly viewing the sun and provide them with certified solar viewing glasses if they wish to observe the eclipse.

6. **Be Mindful of Reflections:** Avoid looking at the sun's reflection in water, glass, or shiny surfaces, as these

can intensify the sun's rays and increase the risk of eye damage.

By following these safety precautions, you can enjoy the spectacle of a solar eclipse while safeguarding your vision and the vision of others.

Protective Eyewear and Viewing Methods:

Protective eyewear is essential for safely viewing a solar eclipse and protecting your eyes from the sun's harmful rays. Here are some recommended viewing methods and types of protective eyewear:

1. **Solar Viewing Glasses:** Solar viewing glasses are specially designed to filter out harmful ultraviolet, visible, and infrared radiation from the sun. These glasses feature lenses that meet the ISO 12312-2 safety standard, ensuring that they provide adequate protection for observing solar phenomena, including eclipses. When purchasing solar viewing glasses, ensure that they are from a reputable manufacturer and display the ISO certification label.

2. **Welding Glasses:** Welding glasses with shade number 14 or higher can also be used for safely viewing a solar eclipse. These glasses offer sufficient protection against the sun's intense brightness and should be certified for solar viewing purposes. However, not all welding glasses are suitable for solar viewing, so it's essential to verify that they meet the necessary safety standards.

3. **Telescopes and Binoculars:** If you plan to use telescopes or binoculars for observing the eclipse,

ensure that they are equipped with solar filters specifically designed for solar viewing. Solar filters should be securely attached to the front of the optical device to block harmful radiation from the sun. Never look directly at the sun through unfiltered telescopes or binoculars, as this can cause irreversible eye damage.

4. **Pinhole Projectors:** Pinhole projectors offer a safe and simple way to observe a solar eclipse without directly viewing the sun. To create a pinhole projector, poke a small hole in a piece of cardboard and hold it up to

the sun, allowing the sunlight to pass through the hole and project an image onto a surface below. You can also use a telescope or binoculars to project the sun's image onto a white screen or wall.

5. **Solar Filters for Cameras:** If you plan to photograph the eclipse, ensure that your camera is equipped with a solar filter specifically designed for solar photography. Solar filters should be securely attached to the front of the camera lens to block harmful radiation from the sun. Never point your camera directly at the sun without proper solar

filters, as this can damage your camera's sensor and lens.

When selecting protective eyewear or viewing methods for observing a solar eclipse, prioritize safety and ensure that you are using certified equipment that meets the necessary safety standards. By taking precautions and following recommended guidelines, you can enjoy the spectacle of a solar eclipse while protecting your eyes and vision from harm.

ECLIPSE PHOTOGRAPHY TIPS

Equipment Needed:

Photographing a solar eclipse requires specific equipment to ensure both safety and quality of the captured images. Here's a breakdown of the essential equipment needed for eclipse photography:

1. **Digital Single-Lens Reflex (DSLR) Camera:** A DSLR camera is the preferred choice for eclipse photography due to its versatility, manual controls, and interchangeable lenses. However, mirrorless cameras

and advanced compact cameras with manual shooting modes can also be used effectively.

2. **Telephoto Lens:** A telephoto lens with a focal length of at least 200mm is recommended for capturing detailed shots of the sun during the eclipse. Longer focal lengths, such as 300mm or 400mm, allow for even closer views of the sun's surface and any solar phenomena, such as sunspots or prominences.

3. **Solar Filter:** The most critical piece of equipment for eclipse

photography is a solar filter specifically designed for camera lenses. Solar filters block harmful ultraviolet, visible, and infrared radiation from the sun, allowing you to safely photograph the eclipse without damaging your camera sensor or lens. Baader solar film or specialized solar filter sheets are commonly used for this purpose.

4. **Sturdy Tripod:** A sturdy tripod is essential for stabilizing your camera and lens setup, especially when using telephoto lenses or capturing long-exposure shots. Choose a tripod with

adjustable legs and a solid construction to ensure stability and minimize camera shake during the shoot.

5. **Remote Shutter Release:** Using a remote shutter release or intervalometer helps minimize camera shake by allowing you to trigger the camera's shutter without physically touching it. This is particularly useful for capturing long-exposure shots or time-lapse sequences during the eclipse.

6. **Lens Hood:** A lens hood helps reduce lens flare and unwanted reflections caused by stray light entering the lens from oblique angles. Attach a lens hood to your telephoto lens to improve contrast and image quality when photographing the sun.

7. **Lens Cleaning Kit:** Keep a lens cleaning kit handy to remove dust, smudges, or fingerprints from your camera lens before and during the eclipse shoot. Clean lenses ensure optimal image quality and clarity in your photos.

8. **Backup Batteries and Memory Cards:** Make sure to carry spare camera batteries and memory cards to avoid running out of power or storage space during the eclipse shoot. Cold temperatures or prolonged use can drain battery life quickly, so be prepared with backups.

Techniques for Capturing Stunning Photos:

Once you have the necessary equipment assembled, here are some techniques and tips for capturing stunning photos of the solar eclipse:

1. **Preparation and Planning:** Familiarize yourself with the eclipse path, timing, and weather conditions in advance to choose the best location for your shoot. Arrive early at your chosen location to set up your equipment and ensure everything is in working order.

2. **Composition:** Experiment with different compositions and framing techniques to capture visually compelling images of the eclipse. Include elements such as landscapes, silhouettes, or architectural structures

to add context and interest to your photos.

3. **Exposure Settings:** Use manual exposure mode on your camera to adjust settings such as aperture, shutter speed, and ISO sensitivity for optimal exposure during the eclipse. Start with a low ISO setting (e.g., ISO 100) and narrow aperture (e.g., f/8 to f/16) to maintain sharpness and detail in your photos.

4. **Focus:** Achieving sharp focus is critical for capturing detailed images of the sun during the eclipse. Use

manual focus mode on your camera and set the focus to infinity, then fine-tune the focus manually to ensure crisp, clear images.

5. **Bracketing:** Consider using exposure bracketing to capture a series of photos at different exposure levels, especially during the various phases of the eclipse (e.g., partial, total). This technique allows you to blend multiple exposures later in post-processing to enhance dynamic range and detail in your photos.

6. **Filters and Accessories:** Experiment with different types of solar filters, such as neutral density filters or polarizing filters, to enhance contrast and reduce glare in your eclipse photos. Additionally, consider using accessories like lens hoods or lens caps to further minimize lens flare and unwanted reflections.

7. **Long-Exposure Techniques:** Explore long-exposure photography techniques to capture unique and creative images of the eclipse, such as starburst effects or light trails. Use a sturdy tripod and remote shutter

release to minimize camera shake during long exposures.

8. **Experimentation and Creativity:** Don't be afraid to experiment with different camera angles, perspectives, and shooting techniques to capture distinctive and memorable images of the eclipse. Embrace creativity and spontaneity in your photography to create truly stunning eclipse photos.

By following these tips and techniques, you can capture breathtaking images of the solar eclipse that showcase the beauty and wonder of this celestial event. Remember to prioritize safety at all times and enjoy the experience of photographing one of nature's most awe-inspiring phenomena.

HISTORICAL AND CULTURAL SIGNIFICANCE

Myths and Legends Surrounding Solar Eclipses:

Throughout history, solar eclipses have inspired awe, fear, and wonder among various cultures around the world, leading to the creation of myths, legends, and folklore to explain these celestial phenomena. Here are some notable myths and legends surrounding solar eclipses:

1. **The Dragon Devouring the Sun:** In many ancient cultures, solar eclipses were interpreted as the sun being devoured by a celestial dragon or serpent. People would make loud noises, beat drums, or shoot arrows into the sky to scare away the dragon and ensure the sun's return.

2. **Conflict Between Sun and Moon Deities:** In some mythologies, solar eclipses were seen as symbolic of a conflict or battle between solar and lunar deities. For example, in Norse mythology, the god Odin's wolves were believed to chase the sun and moon,

occasionally catching them and causing eclipses.

3. **Displeasure of Gods:** In certain cultures, solar eclipses were viewed as omens of divine displeasure or impending doom. Eclipse events were often accompanied by rituals, prayers, or sacrifices to appease the gods and ward off calamity.

4. **Temporary Darkness or End of the World:** In ancient civilizations such as the Maya, solar eclipses were sometimes interpreted as signs of impending apocalypse or the end of

the world. Fear and uncertainty surrounding eclipses led to widespread panic and ritualistic responses to ensure survival.

5. **Symbolism of Transformation or Renewal:** Despite the fear associated with solar eclipses, some cultures saw them as symbols of transformation, renewal, or rebirth. Eclipses were viewed as opportunities for spiritual growth, personal reflection, and embracing change.

While these myths and legends may seem outdated or superstitious in modern times, they reflect humanity's enduring fascination with celestial events and our attempts to understand and interpret the mysteries of the cosmos.

Historical Observations and Discoveries:

Solar eclipses have played a significant role in shaping our understanding of astronomy, physics, and the natural world throughout history. Here are some key historical observations and discoveries associated with solar eclipses:

1. **Predictive Capabilities:** Ancient civilizations such as the Babylonians, Greeks, and Mayans made early attempts to predict the occurrence of solar eclipses based on celestial observations and mathematical calculations. These early predictions laid the foundation for modern eclipse forecasting and astronomical understanding.

2. **Verification of Einstein's Theory of General Relativity:** One of the most famous examples of the scientific significance of solar eclipses

occurred in 1919 when British astronomer Sir Arthur Eddington observed a solar eclipse to test Albert Einstein's theory of general relativity. Eddington's observations of starlight bending around the sun during the eclipse provided crucial evidence supporting Einstein's revolutionary theory.

3. **Study of the Sun's Corona:** Solar eclipses offer unique opportunities to study the sun's outer atmosphere, known as the corona, which is typically obscured by the sun's glare. During a total solar eclipse, the moon's shadow

reveals the corona's structure, dynamics, and magnetic fields, providing valuable insights into solar physics and space weather phenomena.

4. **Cultural and Historical Records:** Solar eclipses have been documented in various historical and cultural records, including ancient manuscripts, artwork, and oral traditions. These records not only provide insights into ancient perceptions of eclipses but also serve as valuable historical artifacts for

studying past civilizations and their scientific knowledge.

5. **Inspiration for Scientific Exploration:** Solar eclipses continue to inspire scientific research and exploration, with modern astronomers and space agencies leveraging advanced technologies to study eclipses from space, ground-based observatories, and specialized research aircraft. These efforts contribute to ongoing advancements in solar science, space weather forecasting, and understanding the sun-earth connection.

Overall, solar eclipses have left an indelible mark on human history, culture, and scientific progress, serving as windows into the mysteries of the universe and fueling humanity's curiosity and quest for knowledge.

CITIZEN SCIENCE OPPORTUNITIES

Contributing to Scientific Research During Eclipses:

Solar eclipses provide unique opportunities for citizen scientists to contribute to scientific research and discoveries. By participating in eclipse-related projects and initiatives, observers can collect valuable data, contribute to scientific understanding, and engage in hands-on learning experiences. Here are some ways citizen scientists can contribute to scientific research during eclipses:

1. **Photometric Measurements:** Citizen scientists equipped with specialized photometric equipment, such as photometers or CCD cameras, can capture precise measurements of the sun's brightness before, during, and after a solar eclipse. These measurements help researchers study changes in solar irradiance and atmospheric conditions during the eclipse, contributing to our understanding of solar physics and Earth's atmosphere.

2. **Temperature Monitoring:** Observers can record temperature changes during a solar eclipse using handheld thermometers or weather stations. By documenting variations in ambient temperature before, during, and after the eclipse, citizen scientists contribute data to studies of atmospheric dynamics, thermal effects, and climate patterns.

3. **Animal and Plant Behavior Studies:** Citizen scientists can observe and document animal and plant behavior during a solar eclipse to

study potential effects of changes in light and temperature on biological organisms. Observations of animal movements, vocalizations, or plant responses provide insights into circadian rhythms, ecological dynamics, and environmental adaptation strategies.

4. **Radio Propagation Studies:** Amateur radio operators can participate in radio propagation experiments during a solar eclipse, monitoring changes in radio wave propagation and signal strength at different frequencies. These

experiments help researchers study ionospheric disturbances, radio wave absorption, and atmospheric effects on radio communications.

5. **Airborne Observations:** Citizen scientists with access to small aircraft or drones can conduct airborne observations of the eclipse from unique vantage points, capturing aerial imagery and atmospheric data. These observations complement ground-based measurements and provide additional insights into eclipse phenomena and atmospheric dynamics.

Projects and Initiatives for Eclipse Observers:

Several projects and initiatives engage citizen scientists in eclipse-related research, education, and outreach efforts. These projects offer opportunities for individuals of all ages and backgrounds to participate in eclipse observations and contribute to scientific discovery. Here are some notable projects and initiatives for eclipse observers:

1. **The Citizen CATE Experiment:**
The Citizen Continental-America Telescopic Eclipse (CATE) Experiment is a collaborative project that recruits volunteer citizen scientists to operate a network of identical telescopes along the path of totality during a solar eclipse. Participants capture images and videos of the eclipse's inner corona, providing valuable data for studying solar dynamics and coronal structure.

2. **GLOBE Observer Eclipse App:**
The Global Learning and Observations to Benefit the Environment (GLOBE)

Observer program offers a mobile app that allows citizen scientists to contribute eclipse observations, including temperature measurements, cloud cover observations, and animal behavior data. Participants can upload their observations to the GLOBE database for use in scientific research and analysis.

3. **Eclipse Megamovie Project:** The Eclipse Megamovie Project engages citizen scientists in capturing and sharing images of total solar eclipses to create high-resolution, time-lapse videos of the eclipse's progression.

Participants submit their eclipse photos to be stitched together into a comprehensive megamovie, providing a unique visual record of the eclipse from multiple locations.

4. **Eclipse-related Citizen Science Campaigns:** Various scientific organizations, research institutions, and amateur astronomy groups organize eclipse-related citizen science campaigns and outreach events to encourage public participation in eclipse observations and data collection. These campaigns often provide resources, training, and

educational materials to support citizen scientists in their eclipse-related activities.

5. **Community Science Centers and Observatories:** Community science centers, planetariums, and observatories often host public events and workshops focused on solar eclipses, providing opportunities for hands-on learning, telescope viewing, and citizen science activities. These venues serve as hubs for engaging with the public and promoting scientific literacy around eclipses and astronomy.

By participating in citizen science projects and initiatives during solar eclipses, observers can make meaningful contributions to scientific research, expand their knowledge of astronomy, and inspire future generations of scientists and astronomers. Citizen scientists play a vital role in advancing our understanding of the universe and fostering a culture of scientific inquiry and exploration.

PLANNING YOUR ECLIPSE EXPERIENCE

Travel Tips and Accommodation:

Planning for a solar eclipse experience involves careful consideration of travel logistics, accommodation options, and ensuring a comfortable and enjoyable viewing experience. Here are some tips to help you plan your eclipse adventure:

1. **Book Accommodation Early:** Since solar eclipses attract large crowds of observers, especially in

prime viewing locations along the path of totality, it's essential to book accommodation well in advance. Consider options such as hotels, campgrounds, vacation rentals, or staying with friends or family in nearby areas. Be flexible with your travel dates and consider arriving a day or two before the eclipse to avoid last-minute rush and congestion.

2. **Choose a Viewing Location:** Research and select a suitable viewing location along the path of totality based on factors such as weather forecasts, accessibility, and amenities.

Consider viewing sites with unobstructed views of the horizon and minimal light pollution for optimal viewing conditions. Plan ahead for transportation to and from your chosen viewing site, especially if it requires hiking or off-road travel.

3. **Pack Essential Supplies:** Prepare a checklist of essential supplies and equipment for your eclipse trip, including camping gear, food and water, clothing for varying weather conditions, sunscreen, insect repellent, portable chairs or blankets, and any specialized eclipse viewing

equipment such as solar filters or telescopes. Pack a first-aid kit, flashlight, and emergency supplies for unexpected situations.

4. **Travel Responsibly:** Plan your travel route in advance and allow extra time for potential traffic delays or road closures due to increased eclipse-related traffic. Follow all traffic laws, drive safely, and respect local regulations and guidelines. Consider carpooling or using public transportation to reduce congestion and minimize environmental impact.

5. **Stay Informed:** Monitor weather forecasts and eclipse updates regularly in the days leading up to the event to make informed decisions about your travel plans and viewing location. Be prepared to adjust your itinerary or relocate to alternative viewing sites if weather conditions are unfavorable at your original location. Stay connected with local authorities, event organizers, and fellow eclipse enthusiasts for real-time updates and recommendations.

Weather Considerations and Contingency Plans:

Weather conditions play a crucial role in determining the success of your eclipse viewing experience. Here are some weather considerations and contingency plans to help you prepare for various scenarios:

1. **Check Weather Forecasts:** Monitor weather forecasts for your chosen viewing location and surrounding areas in the days leading up to the eclipse. Pay attention to factors such as cloud cover,

precipitation, wind speed, and visibility to assess the likelihood of clear skies during the eclipse. Use reliable weather forecasting websites, apps, or local meteorological services for up-to-date information.

2. **Have a Backup Plan:** Prepare a backup plan in case of inclement weather or unfavorable viewing conditions at your primary location. Identify alternative viewing sites within driving distance that offer better weather prospects or clearer skies. Be prepared to relocate to these backup sites if necessary, and have

contingency transportation arrangements in place.

3. **Be Flexible:** Stay flexible and adaptable to changing weather conditions and circumstances on the day of the eclipse. If clouds obscure the sun during the partial phases of the eclipse, remain patient and optimistic, as conditions may improve closer to totality. Keep an open mind and be ready to embrace unexpected outcomes or changes to your original viewing plans.

4. **Seek Local Advice:** Seek advice from local residents, astronomers, or experienced eclipse chasers familiar with the area's weather patterns and microclimates. They can provide valuable insights and recommendations for alternative viewing sites or strategies based on their knowledge of the region's weather behavior.

5. **Stay Safe:** Prioritize your safety and well-being during the eclipse experience, especially if adverse weather conditions or unforeseen circumstances arise. Follow all safety

guidelines and instructions from local authorities, event organizers, and experienced observers. Avoid taking unnecessary risks or venturing into hazardous areas in pursuit of the perfect viewing spot.

By planning ahead, staying informed, and remaining flexible, you can maximize your chances of experiencing a memorable and successful solar eclipse viewing adventure, regardless of weather conditions or unforeseen challenges. Remember to enjoy the experience and appreciate the awe-inspiring beauty of nature's celestial spectacle.

POST-ECLIPSE REFLECTIONS

Personal Experiences and Observations:

After witnessing a solar eclipse, many individuals reflect on their personal experiences and observations of this rare celestial event. Here are some common themes and reflections shared by eclipse observers:

1. **Sense of Awe and Wonder:** Witnessing a total solar eclipse often evokes a profound sense of awe and wonder at the beauty and grandeur of

the natural world. Observers describe feeling humbled and inspired by the spectacle of the moon's shadow sweeping across the landscape and the sudden darkness enveloping the surroundings during totality.

2. **Emotional Impact:** Eclipse experiences can evoke a range of emotions, including excitement, anticipation, joy, and even spiritual or transcendent feelings. Observers may feel a deep connection to the universe and a sense of unity with other participants in the shared experience of witnessing the eclipse.

3. **Scientific Curiosity:** For many observers, solar eclipses spark a renewed interest in astronomy, science, and space exploration. Witnessing the eclipse firsthand may inspire individuals to learn more about celestial phenomena, planetary dynamics, and the broader universe, leading to further exploration and study.

4. **Community and Camaraderie:** Eclipse events often bring together diverse groups of people, fostering a sense of community and camaraderie

among participants. Observers share stories, swap eclipse viewing tips, and bond over their shared enthusiasm for astronomy and celestial events.

5. **Memorable Moments:** Eclipse experiences create lasting memories that individuals cherish for a lifetime. Whether it's the breathtaking beauty of the sun's corona during totality, the eerie darkness of the eclipse's shadow, or the collective excitement of the crowd, eclipse observers often recount specific moments that leave a lasting impression.

Impacts on Local Communities and Tourism:

Solar eclipses can have significant impacts on local communities and tourism economies, especially in areas along the path of totality. Here are some key reflections on the impacts of eclipses on local communities:

1. **Economic Boost:** Eclipse events attract thousands of visitors to communities along the path of totality, providing a significant economic boost to local businesses, restaurants, hotels, and tourism-related activities. Eclipse-

related tourism generates revenue for hotels, restaurants, souvenir shops, and other businesses, stimulating economic growth and development in the region.

2. **Infrastructure and Services:** Local communities must prepare for the influx of visitors by upgrading infrastructure, increasing public safety measures, and providing essential services such as transportation, accommodations, and emergency medical care. These preparations require coordination and collaboration among government agencies,

community organizations, and local businesses to ensure a smooth and enjoyable experience for eclipse visitors.

3. **Cultural and Educational Opportunities:** Solar eclipses offer unique cultural and educational opportunities for local communities to showcase their history, heritage, and natural beauty to visitors from around the world. Communities may organize eclipse-related events, festivals, and educational programs to engage visitors and promote awareness of

local culture, traditions, and environmental conservation efforts.

4. **Environmental Impact:** Eclipse events can have environmental impacts on local ecosystems, wildlife habitats, and natural resources due to increased human activity, waste generation, and habitat disturbance. Local communities must balance the economic benefits of eclipse tourism with environmental conservation efforts to minimize negative impacts on the environment and preserve the region's natural beauty for future generations.

5. **Legacy and Legacy Planning:**
Solar eclipses leave a lasting legacy on local communities, creating memories and experiences that endure long after the event has passed. Communities may develop legacy projects and initiatives to commemorate the eclipse, such as public art installations, educational programs, or community resources that celebrate the cultural and scientific significance of the event.

Overall, solar eclipses offer valuable opportunities for personal reflection, scientific discovery, and community engagement, leaving a lasting impact on individuals, communities, and the broader society. By embracing the unique experiences and opportunities presented by eclipses, communities can harness their potential to inspire, educate, and unite people from all walks of life.

FUTURE ECLIPSES AND CONCLUSION

Upcoming Solar Eclipses Around the World:

As celestial events that captivate people's imaginations and inspire awe, solar eclipses continue to draw attention and anticipation from skywatchers around the world. Here are some upcoming solar eclipses to look forward to:

1. **June 13, 2132:** A total solar eclipse will occur over the Arctic region, with

the path of totality crossing Greenland, Iceland, and the North Atlantic Ocean. This eclipse offers a rare opportunity to witness totality within the remote and pristine landscapes of the Arctic Circle.

2. **August 2, 2027:** A total solar eclipse will sweep across North Africa, the Middle East, and Central Asia, providing spectacular views for observers in countries such as Morocco, Spain, Algeria, Libya, Egypt, Saudi Arabia, and India. This eclipse offers a unique blend of cultural heritage, historical landmarks, and

natural beauty along its path of totality.

3. **August 12, 2026:** A total solar eclipse will sweep across the United States, with the path of totality stretching from the Pacific Northwest to the Southeastern states. This eclipse, often referred to as the "Great North American Eclipse," follows a similar path to the historic 2017 total solar eclipse, providing another chance for millions of Americans to witness totality.

Final Thoughts and Recommendations:

Solar eclipses are extraordinary cosmic events that remind us of the beauty, mystery, and interconnectedness of the universe. As we reflect on the past, present, and future of eclipse experiences, here are some final thoughts and recommendations:

1. **Embrace the Wonder:** Whether you're a seasoned eclipse chaser or witnessing your first solar eclipse, embrace the wonder and magic of the experience. Take time to appreciate

the rare celestial alignment that allows us to witness the sun's corona, the moon's shadow, and the beauty of totality.

2. **Share the Experience:** Eclipse events offer opportunities for shared experiences and collective awe. Share your eclipse photos, videos, and stories with friends, family, and fellow enthusiasts to spread awareness and appreciation for these celestial phenomena.

3. **Support Science and Education:** Solar eclipses serve as

valuable opportunities for scientific research, education, and public outreach. Support organizations, museums, and educational institutions that promote astronomy, space science, and STEM education initiatives to inspire future generations of scientists and astronomers.

4. **Practice Safety:** Always prioritize safety when observing solar eclipses. Use certified solar viewing glasses or other approved viewing methods to protect your eyes from harmful solar radiation. Follow safety guidelines and recommendations from experts to

ensure a safe and enjoyable eclipse experience.

5. **Look to the Future:** As we look ahead to future solar eclipses and celestial events, let us continue to nurture our curiosity, wonder, and appreciation for the wonders of the universe. Whether observing from near or far, let us come together as a global community to celebrate the beauty and majesty of the cosmos.

In conclusion, solar eclipses are timeless reminders of the vastness and complexity of the cosmos, offering moments of awe, inspiration, and reflection for people around the world. As we anticipate future eclipses and celestial events, let us cherish the memories and experiences of past eclipses while embracing the excitement and wonder of what lies ahead in the ever-changing tapestry of the universe.